What's Cooking

baking

What's Cooking
baking

A collection of must-have recipes for all occasions

First published in 2010 for Index Books Ltd

LOVE FOOD is an imprint of Parragon Books Ltd

Parragon
Queen Street House
4 Queen Street
Bath BA1 1HE, UK

ISBN: 978-1-4454-0316-8

Printed in China

Cover design by Talking Design
Cover image by Clive Streeter
Internal design by Simon Levy
Additional photography by Clive Streeter
Food styling by Angela Drake and Teresa Goldfinch
Introduction and additional recipes by Christine France

Notes for the Reader
This book uses both metric and imperial measurements. Follow the same units of
measurement throughout; do not mix metric and imperial. All spoon measurements are
level: teaspoons are assumed to be 5 ml, and tablespoons are assumed to be 15 ml.
Unless otherwise stated, milk is assumed to be full fat, eggs and individual vegetables are
medium, and pepper is freshly ground black pepper.

The times given are an approximate guide only. Preparation times differ according to the
techniques used by different people and the cooking times may also vary from those given.
Optional ingredients, variations or serving suggestions have not been included in the
calculations.

Recipes using raw or very lightly cooked eggs should be avoided by infants, the elderly,
pregnant women, convalescents and anyone suffering from an illness. Pregnant and
breastfeeding women are advised to avoid eating peanuts and peanut products. Sufferers
from nut allergies should be aware that some of the ready-made ingredients used in the
recipes in this book may contain nuts. Always check the packaging before use.

CONTENTS

INTRODUCTION

Few types of cookery offer more rewards than home baking. Not only can you make irresistible sweet and savoury treats for your family and friends, but the actual hands-on process of baking is immensely satisfying, and you may be surprised at how much fun it can be. The basic skills are really easy to learn and you need very little in the way of special equipment to make some impressive cakes and bakes. All it needs is a little practice, and you'll get your baking confidence in no time!

While it's true that you can buy good-quality ready-made cakes these days, the satisfaction of baking your own, knowing exactly what ingredients they contain and even making them cheaper than you can buy them makes all the effort worthwhile. If you have children, baking is a great way to encourage them to start helping in the kitchen, and most children love to cook. Even toddlers can usually be given a simple job, as long as they're supervised by an adult. Try starting them off with an easy task like spooning mixture from a bowl into bun cases, for example, or arranging sweet decorations on top of a finished cake.

What's Cooking Baking contains all the recipes you need to enjoy baking, including some familiar classics and lots of new ideas too. You'll find recipes for a huge variety of cakes and bakes – including simple sponge cakes, special occasion cakes and gateaux, delicious desserts, irresistible biscuits, tempting traybakes and buns, sweet and savoury pies and tarts, classic breads and more unusual yeasted bakes with international flavours. All the recipes are thoroughly tested, with easy-to-follow instructions, so you can rely on them for good results every time. Every recipe is illustrated with a beautiful full-colour photograph to get your taste buds going even before you start. If you're just a beginner, you'll find that the comprehensive introduction is packed with invaluable information to get you started, not to mention some useful tips to help you along the way. So now there's no excuse – you have everything you need to start baking!

GETTING STARTED

Choosing bakeware

If you bake regularly, it helps to have a basic selection of cake tins.

- Baking trays – with and without lip

- Deep round and square tins, 18–23 cm/ 7–9 inches

- 2–3 shallow round sandwich tins, 18–20-cm/7–8 inches

- Rectangular traybake tin, about 20 x 30 cm/ 8 x 12 inches

- Round springform tin, 20–23 cm/8–9 inches

- Loaf tins – 450 g/1 lb and 900 g/2 lb

- 12-cup muffin tin

- 12-cup shallow bun tin

- Loose-based tart tin, 20–23 cm/8–9 inches

Fancy tins such as ring tins, Madeleine tins or Bundt tins can be added as required.

Successful baking needs good-quality bakeware that will conduct the heat efficiently and evenly to cake mixtures and will last for years without rusting or warping. Stainless steel tins are long-lasting and will not warp, while aluminium is cheaper but less durable. Non-stick tins can make for easy turning out, but they may not be as durable as uncoated tins. Flexible silicone bakeware is a good alternative to traditional metal tins, but can be expensive.

Why it's important to use the correct tin

If possible, always use the tin size stated in the recipe, as cooking times have been calculated for the stated tin, and if you change it to a very different tin the cake may cook unevenly and give a disappointing result.

What to do if you don't have the correct tin

If you don't have the right tin for the recipe, you don't necessarily have to rush out and buy a new one. Unless it's a particularly unusual shape, most cake tins can be changed for one of the same capacity without harm.

If the recipe uses a round tin but you prefer to use a square one, the square tin should be 2.5 cm/1 inch smaller than the round one. So if the recipe calls for a 23-cm/9-inch round tin, you can substitute a 20-cm/8-inch square one.

GREASING & LINING TINS

Not all cake tins need to be fully lined for baking. For many simple sponges you just need to give the base and sides of the tin a quick brush of oil or melted butter and insert a piece of non-stick baking paper in the base. Richer or low-fat mixtures usually need a thoroughly greased and lined tin to prevent sticking.

Lining a round tin

1 Grease the tin. Cut a strip of baking parchment about 2.5 cm/1 inch longer than the circumference and about 2.5 cm/ 1 inch deeper than the tin.

2 Fold up one long edge about 1 cm/^{1}/$_2$ inch, then unfold leaving a crease.

3 Use scissors to snip cuts along the folded edge of the paper, so that it can be eased into the tin to fit around the curve at the base.

4 Place the tin on a sheet of baking paper and draw around it with a pencil to mark the size. Cut with scissors just inside the line, making a round to fit inside the base, covering the snipped edges of the side lining paper. Grease the paper.

Lining a square tin

1 Grease the tin. Cut a strip of baking parchment about 2.5 cm/1 inch longer than the circumference of the tin and 2.5 cm/ 1 inch deeper.

2 Fold up one long edge about 1 cm/^{1}/$_2$ inch, then unfold leaving a crease. Fit the paper into the sides of the tin, cutting a diagonal slit into the folded edge to fit each corner.

3 Place the tin on a sheet of baking paper, draw around it to mark the size, then cut just inside the line to make a square. Lay the square inside the tin, covering the folded edges. Grease the paper.

Lining a Swiss roll tin or traybake tin

1 Grease the base and sides of the tin. Cut a piece of baking paper 7 cm/2^3/$_4$ inches larger than the tin.

2 Place the tin on the paper, then make a cut from each corner of the paper in towards the tin corner.

3 Place the paper inside the tin so that the diagonally cut corners overlap and fit neatly. Grease the paper.

Lining a loaf tin

1 Grease the tin. Cut a strip of baking paper the length of the tin base and wide enough to cover the base and long sides. Place the paper in the tin.

2 Cut a second piece of parchment the width of the tin base and long enough to cover the base and ends of the tin. Slot this in over the first piece to line the tin, then grease the paper.

Flouring tins

1 Grease the base and sides of the tin, then slip a piece of non-stick baking paper in the base. Grease the paper.

2 Sprinkle a little flour into the tin. Tilt the tin, tapping lightly, so the flour coats the base and sides evenly. Tip out any excess.

EVERYDAY CAKES

VICTORIA SPONGE CAKE

Preheat the oven to 180°C/350°F/Gas Mark 4. Grease and line the bases of two 20-cm/8-inch sandwich tins.

Sift the flour and baking powder into a bowl and add the butter, sugar and eggs. Mix together, then beat well until smooth.

Divide the mixture evenly between the prepared tins and smooth the surfaces. Bake in the preheated oven for 25–30 minutes, or until well risen and golden brown, and the cakes feel springy when lightly pressed.

Leave to cool in the tins for 5 minutes, then turn out and peel off the lining paper. Transfer to wire racks to cool completely. Sandwich the cakes together with the raspberry jam, whipped double cream and strawberry halves. Dust with icing sugar and serve.

SERVES 8

175 g/6 oz self-raising flour

1 tsp baking powder

175 g/6 oz butter, softened, plus extra for greasing

175 g/6 oz golden caster sugar

3 eggs

icing sugar, for dusting

filling

3 tbsp raspberry jam

300 ml/10 fl oz double cream, whipped

16 fresh strawberries, halved

CHOCOLATE
FUDGE CAKE

Preheat the oven to 180°C/350°F/Gas Mark 4. Grease and line the bases of two 20-cm/8-inch sandwich tins.

To make the icing, place the chocolate, muscovado sugar, butter, evaporated milk and vanilla extract in a heavy-based saucepan. Heat gently, stirring constantly, until melted. Pour into a bowl and leave to cool. Cover and chill in the refrigerator for 1 hour, or until spreadable.

For the cake, place the butter and caster sugar in a bowl and beat together until light and fluffy. Gradually beat in the eggs. Stir in the golden syrup and ground almonds. Sift the flour, salt and cocoa powder into a separate bowl, then fold into the mixture. Add a little water, if necessary, to make a dropping consistency.

Spoon the mixture into the prepared tins and bake in the preheated oven for 30–35 minutes, or until springy to the touch and a skewer inserted in the centre comes out clean.

Leave the cakes in the tins for 5 minutes, then turn out onto wire racks to cool completely. When the cakes are cold, sandwich them together with half the icing. Spread the remaining icing over the top and sides of the cake, swirling it to give a frosted appearance.

SERVES 8

175 g/6 oz unsalted butter, softened, plus extra for greasing

175 g/6 oz golden caster sugar

3 eggs, beaten

3 tbsp golden syrup

40 g/1½ oz ground almonds

175 g/6 oz self-raising flour

pinch of salt

40 g/1½ oz cocoa powder

icing

225 g/8 oz plain chocolate, broken into pieces

55 g/2 oz dark muscovado sugar

225 g/8 oz unsalted butter, diced

5 tbsp evaporated milk

½ tsp vanilla extract

COFFEE & WALNUT CAKE

Preheat the oven to 180°C/350°F/Gas Mark 4. Grease and line the bases of two 20-cm/8-inch sandwich tins.

Cream together the butter and muscovado sugar until pale and fluffy. Gradually add the eggs, beating well after each addition. Beat in the coffee.

Sift the flour and baking powder into the mixture, then fold in lightly and evenly with a metal spoon. Fold in the walnut pieces.

Divide the mixture between the prepared cake tins and smooth level. Bake in the preheated oven for 20–25 minutes, or until golden brown and springy to the touch. Turn out onto a wire rack to cool.

For the frosting, beat together the butter, icing sugar, coffee and vanilla extract, mixing until smooth and creamy.

Use about half the mixture to sandwich the cakes together, then spread the remaining frosting on top and swirl with a palette knife. Decorate with walnut halves.

SERVES 8

175 g/6 oz unsalted butter, plus extra for greasing

175 g/6 oz light muscovado sugar

3 large eggs, beaten

3 tbsp strong black coffee

175 g/6 oz self-raising flour

1½ tsp baking powder

115 g/4 oz walnut pieces

walnut halves, to decorate

frosting

115 g/4 oz unsalted butter

200 g/7 oz icing sugar

1 tbsp strong black coffee

½ tsp vanilla extract

MADEIRA CAKE

Preheat the oven to 160°C/325°F/Gas Mark 3. Grease and line an 18-cm/7-inch round deep cake tin.

Cream together the butter and sugar until pale and fluffy. Add the lemon rind and gradually beat in the eggs. Sift in the flours and fold in evenly, adding enough brandy to make a soft dropping consistency.

Spoon the mixture into the prepared tin and smooth the surface. Lay the slices of citron peel on top of the cake.

Bake in the preheated oven for 1–1¼ hours, or until well risen, golden brown and springy to the touch.

Cool in the tin for 10 minutes, then turn out and cool completely on a wire rack.

SERVES 8–10

175 g/6 oz unsalted butter, plus extra for greasing

175 g/6 oz caster sugar

finely grated rind of 1 lemon

3 large eggs, beaten

115 g/4 oz plain flour

115 g/4 oz self-raising flour

2–3 tbsp brandy or milk

2 slices of citron peel

CLASSIC
CHERRY CAKE

Preheat the oven to 180°C/350°F/Gas Mark 4. Grease a 20-cm/ 8-inch round cake tin and line the base and sides with non-stick baking paper.

Stir together the cherries, ground almonds and 1 tablespoon of the flour. Sift the remaining flour into a separate bowl with the baking powder.

Cream together the butter and sugar until light in colour and fluffy in texture. Gradually add the eggs, beating hard with each addition, until evenly mixed.

Add the flour mixture and fold lightly and evenly into the creamed mixture with a metal spoon. Add the cherry mixture and fold in evenly. Finally, fold in the lemon rind and juice.

Spoon the mixture into the prepared cake tin and sprinkle with the crushed sugar cubes. Bake in the preheated oven for 1–1¼ hours, or until risen, golden brown and the cake is just beginning to shrink away from the sides of the tin.

Cool in the tin for about 15 minutes, then turn out to finish cooling on a wire rack.

SERVES 8

250 g/9 oz glacé cherries, quartered

85 g/3 oz ground almonds

200 g/7 oz plain flour

1 tsp baking powder

200 g/7 oz unsalted butter, plus extra for greasing

200 g/7 oz caster sugar

3 large eggs

finely grated rind and juice of 1 lemon

6 sugar cubes, crushed

DEVIL'S FOOD
CAKE

Preheat the oven to 160°C/325°F/Gas Mark 3. Grease two 20-cm/ 8-inch sandwich tins and line the bases with non-stick baking paper.

Break up the chocolate and place with the milk and cocoa powder in a heatproof bowl over a saucepan of hot water, then heat gently, stirring, until melted and smooth. Remove from the heat.

In a large bowl beat together the butter and muscovado sugar until pale and fluffy. Beat in the egg yolks, then the soured cream and the melted chocolate mixture. Sift in the flour and bicarbonate of soda, then fold in evenly. In a separate bowl, whisk the egg whites until stiff enough to hold firm peaks. Fold into the mixture lightly and evenly.

Divide the mixture between the prepared cake tins, smooth level and bake in the preheated oven for 35–40 minutes, or until risen and firm to the touch. Cool in the tins for 10 minutes, then turn out onto a wire rack.

For the frosting, place the chocolate, cocoa powder, soured cream, golden syrup, butter and water in a saucepan and heat gently, until melted. Remove from the heat and sift in the icing sugar, stirring until smooth. Cool, stirring occasionally, until the mixture begins to thicken and hold its shape.

Split the cakes in half horizontally with a sharp knife, to make four layers. Sandwich the cakes together with about a third of the frosting. Spread the remainder over the top and sides of the cakes, swirling with a palette knife.

SERVES 8–10

140 g/5 oz plain chocolate

100 ml/3½ fl oz milk

2 tbsp cocoa powder

140 g/5 oz unsalted butter, plus extra for greasing

140 g/5 oz light muscovado sugar

3 eggs, separated

4 tbsp soured cream or crème fraîche

200 g/7 oz plain flour

1 tsp bicarbonate of soda

frosting

140 g/5 oz plain chocolate

40 g/1½ oz cocoa powder

4 tbsp soured cream or crème fraîche

1 tbsp golden syrup

40 g/1½ oz unsalted butter

4 tbsp water

200 g/7 oz icing sugar

RICH FRUIT
CAKE

Place the sultanas, raisins, apricots and dates in a large bowl and stir in the rum, orange rind and orange juice. Cover and leave to soak for several hours or overnight.

Preheat the oven to 150°C/300°F/Gas Mark 2. Grease and line a 20-cm/8-inch round deep cake tin.

Cream together the butter and sugar until light and fluffy. Gradually beat in the eggs, beating hard after each addition. Stir in the soaked fruits, mixed peel, glacé cherries, glacé ginger and blanched almonds.

Sift together the flour and mixed spice, then fold lightly and evenly into the mixture. Spoon the mixture into the prepared cake tin and level the surface, making a slight depression in the centre with the back of the spoon.

Bake in the preheated oven for 2¼–2¾ hours, or until the cake is beginning to shrink away from the sides and a skewer inserted into the centre comes out clean. Cool completely in the tin.

Turn out the cake and remove the lining paper. Wrap in greaseproof paper and foil, and store for at least two months before use. To add a richer flavour, prick the cake with a skewer and spoon over a couple of extra tablespoons of rum or brandy, if using, before storing.

SERVES 16

350 g/12 oz sultanas

225 g/8 oz raisins

115 g/4 oz ready-to-eat dried apricots, chopped

85 g/3 oz stoned dates, chopped

4 tbsp dark rum or brandy, plus extra for flavouring (optional)

finely grated rind and juice of 1 orange

225 g/8 oz unsalted butter, plus extra for greasing

225 g/8 oz light muscovado sugar

4 eggs

70 g/2½ oz chopped mixed peel

85 g/3 oz glacé cherries, quartered

25 g/1 oz chopped glacé ginger or stem ginger

40 g/1½ oz blanched almonds, chopped

200 g/7 oz plain flour

1 tsp ground mixed spice

CHOCOLATE & VANILLA MARBLED LOAF

Preheat the oven to 160°C/325°F/Gas Mark 3. Grease a 450-g/ 1-lb loaf tin and line the base with non-stick baking paper. Dust a little flour around the inside of the tin, shaking out the excess.

Break up the chocolate, place in a small heatproof bowl with the milk and set over a saucepan of simmering water. Heat gently until just melted. Remove from the heat.

Cream together the butter and sugar until light and fluffy. Beat in the egg and soured cream. Sift the flour and baking powder over the mixture, then fold in lightly and evenly using a metal spoon.

Spoon half the mixture into a separate bowl and stir in the chocolate mixture. Add the vanilla extract to the plain mixture.

Spoon the chocolate and vanilla mixtures alternately into the prepared loaf tin, swirling lightly with a knife or skewer for a marbled effect. Bake in the preheated oven for 40–45 minutes, or until well-risen and firm to the touch.

Cool in the tin for 10 minutes, then turn out and finish cooling on a wire rack.

SERVES 8

55 g/2 oz plain chocolate

3 tbsp milk

70 g/2½ oz unsalted butter, plus extra for greasing

85 g/3 oz caster sugar

1 egg, beaten

3 tbsp soured cream

115 g/4 oz self-raising flour, plus extra for dusting

½ tsp baking powder

½ tsp vanilla extract

BANANA
LOAF

Preheat the oven to 180°C/350°F/Gas Mark 4. Lightly grease and line a 900-g/2-lb loaf tin.

Sift the flours, sugar, salt and the spices into a large bowl. In a separate bowl mash the bananas with the orange juice, then stir in the eggs and oil. Pour into the dry ingredients and mix well.

Spoon into the prepared tin and bake in the preheated oven for 1 hour. Test to see if the loaf is cooked by inserting a skewer into the centre. If it comes out clean, the loaf is done. If not, bake for a further 10 minutes and test again.

Remove from the oven and leave to cool in the tin. Turn out the loaf, slice and serve.

SERVES 8

butter, for greasing

125 g/4½ oz white self-raising flour

100 g/3½ oz light brown self-raising flour

150 g/5½ oz demerara sugar

pinch of salt

½ tsp ground cinnamon

½ tsp ground nutmeg

2 large ripe bananas, peeled

175 ml/6 fl oz orange juice

2 eggs, beaten

4 tbsp rapeseed oil

BATTENBERG CAKE

EVERYDAY CAKES

Preheat the oven to 180°C/350°F/Gas Mark 4. Grease and line an 18-cm/7-inch shallow square baking tin. Cut a strip of double baking paper and grease it. Use this to divide the tin in half.

Cream the butter and sugar in a mixing bowl until pale and fluffy. Gently beat in the eggs and vanilla extract, gradually adding in the flour. Spoon half the mixture into a separate bowl and colour it with a few drops of food colouring.

Spoon the plain mixture into half the prepared baking tin. Spoon the coloured mixture into the other half of the tin, trying to make the divide as straight as possible. Bake in the preheated oven for 35–40 minutes. Turn out and leave to cool on a wire rack.

When cool, trim the edges and cut the cake portions lengthways in half, making four equal parts. Warm the jam in a small saucepan. Brush two sides of each cake portion with some of the jam and stick them together to give a chequerboard effect.

Knead the marzipan with a few drops of food colouring to colour it a subtle shade of pink. Roll out the marzipan to a rectangle wide enough to wrap around the cake. Brush the outside of the cake with the remaining jam. Place the cake on the marzipan and wrap the marzipan around the cake, making sure that the seam is on one corner of the cake. Trim the edges neatly. Crimp the top edges of the cake, if desired, and sprinkle with sugar.

SERVES 6–8

115 g/4 oz butter or margarine, softened, plus extra for greasing

115 g/4 oz caster sugar, plus extra for sprinkling

2 eggs, lightly beaten

1 tsp vanilla extract

115 g/4 oz self-raising flour, sifted

a few drops of pink edible food colouring

2–3 tbsp apricot jam

300 g/10½ oz marzipan

LEMON POLENTA CAKE

Preheat the oven to 180°C/350°F/Gas Mark 4. Lightly grease a 20-cm/8-inch round deep cake tin and line the base with baking paper.

Beat together the butter and sugar until pale and fluffy. Beat in the lemon rind, lemon juice, eggs and ground almonds. Sift in the polenta and baking powder and stir until evenly mixed.

Spoon the mixture into the prepared tin and spread evenly. Bake in the preheated oven for 30–35 minutes, or until just firm to the touch and golden brown. Remove the cake from the oven and leave to cool in the tin for 20 minutes.

For the syrup, place the lemon juice, sugar and water in a small saucepan. Heat gently, stirring until the sugar has dissolved, then bring to the boil and simmer for 3–4 minutes, or until slightly reduced and syrupy.

Turn out the cake onto a wire cooling rack then drizzle half of the syrup evenly over the surface. Leave to cool completely.

Cut the cake into slices, drizzle the extra syrup over the top and serve with crème fraîche.

SERVES 8

200 g/7 oz unsalted butter, plus extra for greasing

200 g/7 oz caster sugar

finely grated rind and juice of 1 large lemon

3 eggs, beaten

140 g/5 oz ground almonds

100 g/3½ oz quick-cook polenta

1 tsp baking powder

crème fraîche, to serve

syrup
juice of 2 lemons

55 g/2 oz caster sugar

2 tbsp water

ORANGE & POPPY SEED BUNDT CAKE

Preheat the oven to 160°C/325°F/Gas Mark 3. Grease and lightly flour a Bundt ring tin, about 24 cm/9 inches in diameter and with a capacity of approximately 2 litres/3 pints.

Cream together the butter and sugar until pale and fluffy, then add the eggs gradually, beating thoroughly after each addition. Stir in the orange rind and poppy seeds. Sift in the flour and baking powder, then fold in evenly. Add the milk and orange juice, stirring to mix evenly.

Spoon the mixture into the prepared tin and bake in the preheated oven for 45–50 minutes, or until firm and golden brown. Leave to cool in the tin for 10 minutes, then turn out onto a wire rack to cool.

For the syrup, place the sugar and orange juice in a saucepan and heat gently until the sugar melts. Bring to the boil and simmer for about 5 minutes, until reduced and syrupy.

Spoon the syrup over the cake whilst it is still warm. Top with the strips of orange zest and serve warm or cold.

SERVES 10

200 g/7 oz unsalted butter,
  plus extra for greasing

200 g/7 oz golden caster sugar

3 large eggs, beaten

finely grated rind of 1 orange

55 g/2 oz poppy seeds

300 g/10½ oz plain flour,
  plus extra for dusting

2 tsp baking powder

150 ml/5 fl oz milk

125 ml/4 fl oz orange juice

strips of orange zest,
  to decorate

syrup

140 g/5 oz golden caster sugar

150 ml/5 fl oz orange juice

CELEBRATION CAKES

BIRTHDAY LEMON SPONGE CAKE

Preheat the oven to 180°C/350°C/Gas Mark 4. Grease two 20-cm/ 8-inch sandwich tins and line the bases with baking paper.

Cream together the butter and caster sugar until pale and fluffy. Gradually add the eggs, beating well after each addition. Sift in the flour and fold in evenly with a metal spoon. Fold in the lemon rind and milk lightly and evenly.

Spoon the mixture into the prepared tins and bake in the preheated oven for 25–30 minutes, or until golden brown and springy to the touch. Leave the cakes to cool in the tins for 2–3 minutes, then turn out onto a wire rack to finish cooling.

For the butter icing, beat together the butter, icing sugar and lemon juice until smooth. Mix about 3 tablespoons of the butter cream with the lemon curd. Use the lemon curd mixture to sandwich the two cakes together.

Spread about two thirds of the remaining butter icing over the top of the cake, swirling with a palette knife. Spoon the remainder into a piping bag and pipe swirls around the edge of the cake. Add candleholders and birthday candles to finish.

SERVES 8–10

250 g/9 oz unsalted butter, plus extra for greasing

250 g/9 oz golden caster sugar

4 eggs, beaten

250 g/9 oz self-raising flour

finely grated rind of 1 lemon

3 tbsp milk

candleholders and birthday candles, to decorate

butter icing

140 g/5 oz unsalted butter

200 g/7 oz icing sugar

2 tbsp lemon juice or lemon liqueur (Limoncello)

3 tbsp lemon curd

DOTTY CHOCOLATE CHIP CAKE

Preheat the oven to 170°C/325°F/Gas Mark 3. Grease a 20-cm/ 8-inch round cake tin and line the base with baking paper.

Place the margarine, sugar, eggs, flour, baking powder and cocoa powder in a bowl and beat until just smooth. Stir in the chocolate chips, mixing evenly.

Spoon the mixture into the prepared tin and spread the top level. Bake in the preheated oven for 40–45 minutes, until risen and firm to the touch. Leave to cool in the tin for 5 minutes, then turn out and finish cooling completely on a wire rack.

For the icing, place the chocolate, butter and golden syrup in a saucepan over a low heat and stir until just melted and smooth.

Remove from the heat and leave to cool until it begins to thicken enough to leave a trail when the spoon is lifted. Pour the icing over the top of the cake, allowing it to drizzle down the sides. Arrange the sweets over the top of the cake.

SERVES 10

175 g/6 oz soft margarine or spreadable butter, plus extra for greasing

175 g/6 oz caster sugar

3 eggs, beaten

175 g/6 oz plain flour

1 tsp baking powder

2 tbsp cocoa powder

55 g/2 oz white chocolate chips

40 g/1½ oz small coloured sweets, such as Smarties, to decorate

icing

175 g/6 oz milk chocolate or plain chocolate

100 g/3½ oz unsalted butter or margarine

1 tbsp golden syrup

VALENTINE CHOCOLATE HEART CAKE

Preheat the oven to 180°C/350°F/Gas Mark 4. Grease a 20-cm/8-inch heart-shaped tin and line the base with baking paper.

Sift the flour, baking powder and cocoa powder into a large bowl. Beat the eggs with the sugar, oil and single cream. Make a well in the dry ingredients and add the egg mixture, then stir to mix thoroughly, beating to a smooth batter.

Pour the mixture into the prepared tin and bake in the preheated oven for 25–30 minutes, or until risen and firm to the touch. Leave to cool in the tin for 10 minutes, then turn out and finish cooling on a wire rack.

For the filling and topping, place the chocolate and double cream in a saucepan over a low heat and stir until melted. Remove from the heat and stir until the mixture cools slightly and begins to thicken.

Use a sharp knife to cut the cake in half horizontally. Spread the cut surface of each half with the raspberry jam, then top with about 3 tablespoons of the chocolate mixture. Scatter half the raspberries over the base and replace the top, pressing lightly.

Spread the remaining chocolate mixture over the top and sides of the cake, swirling with a palette knife. Top with the remaining raspberries and decorate with mint sprigs.

SERVES 12

175 g/6 oz self-raising flour

2 tsp baking powder

55 g/2 oz cocoa powder

3 eggs

140 g/5 oz light muscovado sugar

150 ml/5 fl oz sunflower oil, plus extra for greasing

150 ml/5 fl oz single cream

fresh mint sprigs, to decorate

filling and topping

225 g/8 oz plain chocolate

250 ml/9 fl oz double cream

200 g/7 oz fresh or frozen raspberries

3 tbsp seedless raspberry jam

TRADITIONAL SIMNEL CAKE

Preheat the oven to 150°C/300°F/Gas Mark 2. Grease and line a 20-cm/8-inch round deep cake tin with baking paper.

Place the butter and sugar in a bowl and cream together with an electric whisk or wooden spoon until pale, light and fluffy. Gradually beat in the eggs, beating hard after each addition.

Sift together the flour, baking powder and mixed spice. Use a large metal spoon to fold into the creamed mixture. Stir in the lemon rind, currants, sultanas and mixed peel, mixing evenly. Spoon half the mixture into the prepared tin and smooth level.

Roll out 250 g/9 oz of the marzipan to a 20-cm/8-inch round and place over the mixture in the tin. Add the remaining cake mixture and smooth level.

Bake the cake in the preheated oven for 2¼–2¾ hours, or until firm and golden and the sides are beginning to shrink away from the tin. Leave to cool in the tin for 30 minutes, then turn out onto a wire rack to finish cooling.

Brush the top of the cake with apricot jam. Roll out two thirds of the remaining marzipan to a round to cover the top of the cake. Use a knife to mark a lattice design in the surface and pinch the edges to decorate.

Roll the remaining marzipan into 11 small balls and arrange around edge of the cake. Place under a hot grill for 30–40 seconds to brown lightly. Cool before storing.

SERVES 16

175 g/6 oz unsalted butter, plus extra for greasing

175 g/6 oz light muscovado sugar

3 eggs, beaten

225 g/8 oz plain flour

½ tsp baking powder

2 tsp ground mixed spice

finely grated rind of 1 small lemon

100 g/3½ oz currants

100 g/3½ oz sultanas

55 g/2 oz chopped mixed peel

700 g/1 lb 9 oz marzipan

3 tbsp apricot jam

ROSE-TOPPED WEDDING MUFFINS

Preheat the oven to 200°C/400°F/Gas Mark 6. Increase the quantity of ingredients according to the number of wedding guests invited, working in double quantities to make 24 muffins each time. Grease the appropriate number of muffin tins or line with paper muffin cases.

Sift together the flour, baking powder and salt into a large bowl. Stir in the caster sugar.

Lightly beat the eggs in a large jug or bowl, then beat in the milk, oil and vanilla extract. Make a well in the centre of the dry ingredients and pour in the beaten liquid ingredients. Stir gently until just combined; do not over-mix.

Spoon the mixture into the prepared muffin tin or tins. Bake in the preheated oven for about 20 minutes, until well risen, golden brown and firm to the touch.

Leave the muffins in the tin or tins for 5 minutes, then transfer to a wire rack and leave to cool. Store the muffins in the freezer until required.

On the day of serving, if using fresh flowers, rinse and leave to dry on kitchen paper. For the icing, sift the icing sugar into a bowl. Add the water and stir until the mixture is smooth and thick enough to coat the back of a wooden spoon. Spoon the icing on top of each muffin then top with a rose petal, rose bud or sugar rose.

MAKES 12

oil or melted butter, for greasing (if using)

280 g/10 oz plain flour

1 tbsp baking powder

⅛ tsp salt

115 g/4 oz caster sugar

2 eggs

250 ml/9 fl oz milk

6 tbsp sunflower oil or 85 g/ 3 oz butter, melted and cooled

1 tsp vanilla extract

12 ready-made sugar roses or fresh rose petals or buds, to decorate

icing

175 g/6 oz icing sugar

3–4 tsp hot water

HALLOWEEN SPIDER'S WEB CAKE

Preheat the oven to 170°C/325°F/Gas Mark 3. Grease an 18-cm/7-inch round cake tin and line the base with baking paper.

Cream together the butter and caster sugar until light and fluffy. Beat in the eggs and milk. Sift in the flour and baking powder, then fold in lightly and evenly using a metal spoon.

Spoon half the mixture into a separate bowl and stir in a few drops of orange food colouring, stirring to mix evenly. Place alternate spoonfuls of the plain and orange mixtures into the prepared cake tin, swirling lightly for a marbled effect. Bake in the preheated oven for 35–40 minutes, or until well-risen and firm to the touch. Leave to cool in the tin for 10 minutes, then turn out and finish cooling on a wire rack.

Reserve about 40 g/1½ oz of the icing and colour it with black food colouring, then colour the remaining icing with orange food colouring. Place the cake on a board or plate and brush the top and sides with apricot jam. Roll out the orange icing on a surface lightly dusted with icing sugar so it is large enough to cover the cake, then lift it onto the cake, smoothing with your hands. Trim the edges at the base, reserving the trimmings.

Place the icing sugar in a bowl and stir in enough water to mix to a paste, adding a few drops of black food colouring. Spoon into a small piping bag fitted with a medium plain nozzle, then pipe a spider's web design over the top of the cake. Shape about half of the black icing into an oval for the spider's body, then shape eight legs from the remaining black icing. Shape two eyes from the orange icing trimmings. Place the spider on the web.

SERVES 8–10

115 g/4 oz unsalted butter, plus extra for greasing

115 g/4 oz caster sugar

2 eggs, beaten

3 tbsp milk

140 g/5 oz self-raising flour

½ tsp baking powder

a few drops of orange edible food colouring

topping

500 g/1 lb 2 oz ready-to-roll icing

a few drops black and orange edible food colourings

2 tbsp apricot jam, warmed

100 g/3½ oz icing sugar, plus extra for dusting

CHRISTMAS SNOWFLAKE MUFFINS

Preheat the oven to 200°C/400°F/Gas Mark 6. Grease a 12-cup muffin tin or line with 12 paper muffin cases.

Sift together the flour, baking powder, allspice and salt into a large bowl. Stir in the brown sugar.

Lightly beat the eggs in a large jug or bowl then beat in the milk and oil. Make a well in the centre of the dry ingredients and pour in the beaten liquid ingredients and mincemeat. Stir gently until just combined; do not over-mix.

Spoon the mixture into the prepared muffin tin. Bake in the preheated oven for about 20 minutes, until well risen, golden brown and firm to the touch.

Leave the muffins in the tin for 5 minutes, then transfer to a wire rack and leave to cool.

Knead the icing until pliable. On a surface dusted with icing sugar, roll out the icing to a thickness of 5 mm/¼ inch. Using a 7-cm/2¾-inch fluted cutter, cut out 12 'snowflakes'.

Heat the apricot jam until runny, then brush over the tops of the muffins. Place a snowflake on top of each one, then decorate with silver dragées.

MAKES 12

oil or melted butter,
   for greasing (optional)

280 g/10 oz plain flour

1 tbsp baking powder

1 tsp allspice

⅛ tsp salt

115 g/4 oz soft dark brown sugar

2 eggs

100 ml/3½ fl oz milk

6 tbsp sunflower oil or 85 g/
   3 oz butter, melted and cooled

200 g/7 oz luxury mincemeat
   with cherries and nuts

450 g/1 lb ready-to-roll icing

icing sugar, for dusting

2½ tsp apricot jam

silver dragées, to decorate

SACHERTORTE

Preheat the oven to 150°C/300°F/Gas Mark 2. Grease and line a 23-cm/9-inch round springform cake tin.

Put the chocolate in a heatproof bowl set over a saucepan of gently simmering water until melted. In a separate bowl, beat the butter and 70 g/2½ oz of the sugar until pale and fluffy. Add the egg yolks and beat well. Add the chocolate in a thin stream, beating well. Sift in the flour and fold it into the mixture. Whisk the egg whites until they stand in soft peaks. Add the remaining sugar and whisk until glossy. Fold half the egg white mixture into the chocolate mixture, then fold in the remainder.

Spoon into the prepared tin and smooth the top. Bake in the preheated oven for 1–1¼ hours, until a skewer inserted into the centre comes out clean. Cool in the tin for 5 minutes, then transfer to a wire rack to cool completely.

To make the icing, melt 175 g/6 oz of the chocolate and beat in the coffee until smooth. Sift in the icing sugar and whisk to give a thick icing. Halve the cake. Spread the jam over the cut edges and sandwich together. Invert the cake on a wire rack. Spoon the icing over the cake and spread to coat the top and sides. Leave to set for 5 minutes, letting any excess drop through the rack. Transfer to a serving plate and leave to set for at least 2 hours.

To decorate, melt the remaining chocolate and spoon into a small piping bag fitted with a fine plain nozzle. Pipe the word 'Sacher' or 'Sachertorte' on top of the cake. Leave to set before serving.

SERVES 10

175 g/6 oz plain chocolate, broken into pieces

140 g/5 oz unsalted butter, plus extra for greasing

140 g/5 oz caster sugar

6 eggs, separated

175 g/6 oz plain flour

icing

225 g/8 oz plain chocolate, broken into pieces

5 tbsp strong black coffee

175 g/6 oz icing sugar

6 tbsp apricot jam, warmed

CHOCOLATE TRUFFLE TORTE

Preheat the oven to 220°C/425°F/Gas Mark 7. Grease and line a 23-cm/9-inch round springform cake tin.

Put the sugar and eggs in a heatproof bowl set over a saucepan of gently simmering water. Whisk together until pale and resembling the texture of mousse. Sift in the flour and cocoa and fold gently into the mixture.

Pour into the prepared tin and bake in the preheated oven for 7–10 minutes, or until risen and firm to the touch. Transfer to a wire rack to cool. Wash and dry the tin and return the cooled cake to the tin. Mix together the coffee and brandy and brush over the cake.

To make the truffle filling, put the cream in a bowl and whisk until just holding very soft peaks. Put the chocolate in a heatproof bowl set over a saucepan of gently simmering water until melted. Carefully fold the cooled melted chocolate into the cream. Pour the chocolate mixture over the sponge. Chill until set.

To decorate the torte, sift cocoa powder over the top and remove carefully from the tin. Using strips of card or baking paper, sift bands of icing sugar over the torte to create a striped pattern. To serve, cut into slices with a hot knife.

SERVES 10

butter, for greasing

55 g/2 oz caster sugar

2 eggs

25 g/1 oz plain flour

25 g/1 oz cocoa powder

4 tbsp strong black coffee

2 tbsp brandy

cocoa powder and icing sugar, to decorate

filling

600 ml/1 pint whipping cream

425 g/15 oz plain chocolate, broken into pieces

RASPBERRY VACHERIN

Preheat the oven to 140°C/275°F/Gas Mark 1. Draw three rectangles, measuring 10 x 25 cm/4 x 10 inches, on sheets of baking paper and place on two baking trays.

Whisk the egg whites in a mixing bowl until soft peaks form, then gradually whisk in half the sugar and continue whisking until the mixture is very stiff and glossy.

Carefully fold in the remaining sugar, the cornflour and the grated chocolate with a metal spoon or a palette knife.

Spoon the meringue mixture into a piping bag fitted with a 1-cm/½-inch plain nozzle and pipe lines across the rectangles.

Bake in the preheated oven for 1½ hours, changing the position of the baking trays halfway through. Without opening the oven door, turn off the oven and leave the meringues to cool inside the oven, then peel away the baking paper.

Place the chocolate in a heatproof bowl set over a saucepan of gently simmering water until melted. Spread the chocolate over two of the meringue layers. Leave to harden.

Place one chocolate-coated meringue on a plate and top with about one third of the cream and raspberries. Gently place the second chocolate-coated meringue on top and spread with half of the remaining cream and raspberries. Place the last meringue on the top and decorate with the remaining cream and raspberries.

Drizzle the melted chocolate over the top of the vacherin and serve.

SERVES 10

3 egg whites

175 g/6 oz caster sugar

1 tsp cornflour

25 g/1 oz plain chocolate, grated

filling & topping

175 g/6 oz plain chocolate, broken into pieces

450 ml/16 fl oz double cream, whipped

280 g/10 oz fresh raspberries

a little melted chocolate, to decorate

STRAWBERRY ROULADE

Preheat the oven to 220°C/425°F/Gas Mark 7. Line a 35 x 25-cm/ 14 x 10-inch Swiss roll tin with baking paper.

Place the eggs in a mixing bowl with the caster sugar. Place the bowl over a saucepan of hot, but not boiling, water and whisk until pale and thick.

Remove the bowl from the pan. Sift in the flour and fold into the egg mixture with the hot water. Pour the mixture into the prepared tin and bake in the preheated oven for about 8–10 minutes, until golden and springy to the touch.

Remove from the tin and transfer to a sheet of baking paper. Peel off the lining paper and roll up the sponge tightly along with the baking paper. Wrap in a clean tea towel and set aside to cool.

For the filling, mix together the fromage frais and almond extract. Cover and chill in the refrigerator until required. Wash, hull and slice the strawberries.

Unroll the sponge, spread the fromage frais mixture over it and sprinkle with the sliced strawberries. Roll the sponge up again (without the baking paper this time) and transfer to a serving plate. Sprinkle with the toasted flaked almonds and serve.

SERVES 8

3 large eggs

125 g/4½ oz caster sugar

125 g/4½ oz plain flour

1 tbsp hot water

1 tbsp toasted flaked almonds, to decorate

filling

200 ml/7 fl oz low-fat fromage frais

1 tsp almond extract

225 g/8 oz small strawberries

BLACK FOREST ROULADE

Preheat the oven to 190°C/375°F/Gas Mark 5. Grease and line a 35 x 25-cm/14 x 10-inch Swiss roll tin.

Break the chocolate into small pieces and place in a heatproof bowl set over a saucepan of gently simmering water. Add the kirsch and heat gently, stirring until the mixture is smooth. Remove from the pan and set aside.

Place the eggs and caster sugar in a large heatproof bowl and set over the pan of gently simmering water. Whisk the eggs and sugar until very thick and creamy and the whisk leaves a trail when dragged across the surface. Remove the bowl from the heat and whisk in the cooled chocolate mixture.

Spoon into the prepared tin, then tap the tin lightly on the work surface to smooth the top. Bake in the preheated oven for 20 minutes, or until firm to the touch. Remove from the oven and immediately invert onto a sheet of baking paper that has been dusted with the icing sugar. Lift off the tin and lining paper, then roll up, encasing the baking paper in the roulade. Leave until cold.

For the filling, whip the cream until soft peaks form, then stir in the kirsch. Unroll the roulade and spread over the cream to within ¼ inch/5 mm of the edges. Scatter the cherries over the cream. Carefully roll up the roulade again and place on a serving platter.

SERVES 8–10

sunflower oil, for greasing

175 g/6 oz plain chocolate

2–3 tbsp kirsch or brandy

5 eggs

225 g/8 oz caster sugar

icing sugar, for dusting

filling

350 ml/12 fl oz double cream

1–2 tbsp kirsch or brandy

350 g/12 oz fresh black cherries, stoned, or 400 g/14 oz canned morello cherries, drained and stoned

BROWNIE BASE
CHEESECAKE

Preheat the oven to 180°C/350°F/Gas Mark 4. Lightly grease and flour a 23-cm/9-inch square cake tin.

Melt the butter and chocolate in a saucepan over a low heat, stirring until smooth. Remove from the heat and beat in the sugar.

Add the eggs and milk, beating well. Stir in the flour, mixing just until blended. Spoon into the prepared tin, spreading evenly.

Bake in the preheated oven for 25 minutes. Remove from the oven and reduce the oven temperature to 160°C/325°F/Gas Mark 3.

For the topping, beat together the cheese, sugar, eggs and vanilla extract until well blended. Stir in the yogurt, then pour over the brownie base. Bake for a further 45–55 minutes, or until the centre is almost set.

Run a knife around the edge of the cheesecake to loosen from the tin. Leave to cool before removing from the tin. Chill in the refrigerator for 4 hours or overnight before cutting into slices. Drizzle with the melted chocolate and serve with chocolate-dipped strawberries.

SERVES 12

brownie base
115 g/4 oz unsalted butter, plus extra for greasing

115 g/4 oz plain chocolate

200 g/7 oz caster sugar

2 eggs, beaten

50 ml/2 fl oz milk

115 g/4 oz plain flour, plus extra for dusting

strawberries dipped in melted chocolate, to serve

topping
500 g/1 lb 2 oz soft cheese

125 g/4½ oz golden caster sugar

3 eggs, beaten

1 tsp vanilla extract

115 g/4 oz natural yogurt

melted chocolate, for drizzling

SMALL CAKES & BARS

LEMON & POPPY SEED MUFFINS

Preheat the oven to 190°C/375°F/Gas Mark 5. Place 12 paper muffin cases in a muffin tin.

Sift the flour and baking powder into a large bowl and stir in the sugar.

Heat a heavy-based frying pan over a medium–high heat and add the poppy seeds, then toast for about 30 seconds, shaking the pan to prevent them burning. Remove from the heat and add to the flour mixture.

Melt the butter, then beat with the egg, milk, lemon rind and lemon juice. Pour into the dry mixture and stir well to mix evenly to a soft, sticky dough. Add a little more milk if the mixture is too dry.

Spoon the mixture into the muffin cases, then bake in the preheated oven for 25–30 minutes, or until risen and golden brown. Place on a wire rack to cool.

MAKES 12

350 g/12 oz plain flour

1 tbsp baking powder

115 g/4 oz caster sugar

2 tbsp poppy seeds

55 g/2 oz unsalted butter

1 large egg, beaten

225 ml/8 fl oz milk

finely grated rind and juice of 1 lemon

DOUBLE CHOCOLATE MUFFINS

Preheat the oven to 190°C/375°F/Gas Mark 5. Place 12 paper muffin cases in a muffin tin.

Put the butter, caster sugar and muscovado sugar into a bowl and beat well. Beat in the eggs, soured cream and milk until thoroughly mixed. Sift the flour, bicarbonate of soda and cocoa powder into a separate bowl and stir into the mixture. Add the chocolate chips and mix well.

Spoon the mixture into the paper cases. Bake in the preheated oven for 25–30 minutes. Remove from the oven and leave to cool for 10 minutes. Turn out onto a wire rack and leave to cool completely.

MAKES 12

100 g/3½ oz butter, softened

125 g/4½ oz caster sugar

100 g/3½ oz dark muscovado sugar

2 eggs

150 ml/5 fl oz soured cream

5 tbsp milk

250 g/9 oz plain flour

1 tsp bicarbonate of soda

2 tbsp cocoa powder

190 g/6½ oz plain chocolate chips

ICED FAIRY
CAKES

Preheat the oven to 190°C/375°F/Gas Mark 5. Place 16 paper bun cases into a shallow bun tin.

Place the butter and caster sugar in a large bowl and cream together with a wooden spoon or electric mixer until pale and fluffy.

Gradually add the eggs, beating well after each addition. Fold in the flour lightly and evenly using a metal spoon.

Divide the mixture evenly between the bun cases and bake in the preheated oven for 15–20 minutes. Cool on a wire rack.

For the icing, sift the icing sugar into a bowl and stir in just enough of the water to mix to a smooth paste that is thick enough to coat the back of a wooden spoon. Stir in a few drops of food colouring, if using. Spread the icing over the fairy cakes and decorate as desired.

MAKES 16

115 g/4 oz unsalted butter, softened

115 g/4 oz caster sugar

2 eggs, beaten

115 g/4 oz self-raising flour

icing and decoration

200 g/7 oz icing sugar

about 2 tbsp warm water

a few drops of edible food colouring (optional)

sugar flowers, hundreds and thousands, glacé cherries, and/or chocolate strands, to decorate

CHOCOLATE BUTTERFLY CAKES

Preheat the oven to 180°C/350°F/Gas Mark 4. Place 12 paper bun cases in a shallow bun tin.

Place the margarine, caster sugar, flour, eggs and cocoa powder in a large bowl, and beat with an electric whisk until the mixture is just smooth. Beat in the melted chocolate.

Spoon the mixture into the paper cases, filling them three-quarters full. Bake in the preheated oven for 15 minutes, or until springy to the touch. Transfer to a wire rack and leave to cool completely.

Meanwhile, make the lemon buttercream. Place the butter in a mixing bowl and beat until fluffy, then gradually beat in the icing sugar. Beat in the lemon rind and gradually add the lemon juice, beating well.

Cut the top off each cake, using a serrated knife. Cut each cake top in half. Spread or pipe the lemon buttercream over the cut surface of each cake and push the two cut pieces of cake top into the icing to form wings. Dust with icing sugar.

MAKES 12

125 g/4½ oz soft margarine

125 g/4½ oz caster sugar

150 g/5½ oz self-raising flour

2 large eggs

2 tbsp cocoa powder

25 g/1 oz plain chocolate, melted

icing sugar, for dusting

lemon buttercream

100 g/3½ oz unsalted butter, softened

225 g/8 oz icing sugar, sifted

grated rind of ½ lemon

1 tbsp lemon juice

DOUBLE CHOCOLATE BROWNIES

Preheat the oven to 180°C/350°F/Gas Mark 4. Grease an 18-cm/ 7-inch square cake tin and line the base with baking paper.

Place the butter and chocolate in a small heatproof bowl set over a saucepan of gently simmering water until melted. Stir until smooth. Leave to cool slightly. Stir in the sugar, salt and vanilla extract. Add the eggs, one at a time, and stir until blended.

Sift the flour and cocoa powder into the mixture and beat until smooth. Stir in the chocolate chips, then pour the mixture into the prepared tin. Bake in the preheated oven for 35–40 minutes, or until the top is evenly coloured and a cocktail stick inserted into the centre comes out almost clean. Leave to cool slightly while you prepare the sauce.

To make the fudge sauce, place the butter, sugar, milk, cream and golden syrup in a small saucepan and heat gently until the sugar has dissolved. Bring to the boil and stir for 10 minutes, or until the mixture is caramel-coloured. Remove from the heat and add the chocolate. Stir until smooth. Cut the brownies into squares and serve immediately with the sauce.

MAKES 9

115 g/4 oz butter, plus extra for greasing

115 g/4 oz plain chocolate, broken into pieces

300 g/10½ oz golden caster sugar

pinch of salt

1 tsp vanilla extract

2 large eggs

140 g/5 oz plain flour

2 tbsp cocoa powder

100 g/3½ oz white chocolate chips

fudge sauce

4 tbsp butter

225 g/8 oz golden caster sugar

150 ml/5 fl oz milk

250 ml/9 fl oz double cream

225 g/8 oz golden syrup

200 g/7 oz plain chocolate, broken into pieces

CAPPUCCINO BROWNIES

Preheat the oven to 180°C/350°F/Gas Mark 4. Grease a 28 x 18-cm/11 x 7-inch shallow cake tin and line the base with baking paper.

Sift the flour, baking powder and cocoa into a bowl and add the butter, caster sugar, eggs and coffee. Beat well, by hand or with an electric whisk, until smooth, then spoon into the prepared tin and smooth the top.

Bake in the preheated oven for 35–40 minutes, or until risen and firm. Leave to cool in the tin for 10 minutes, then turn out onto a wire rack and peel off the lining paper. Leave to cool completely.

To make the frosting, place the chocolate, butter and milk in a bowl set over a saucepan of gently simmering water and stir until the chocolate has melted. Remove the bowl from the pan and sift in the icing sugar. Beat until smooth, then spread over the cake. Dust the top of the cake with cocoa powder, then cut into squares.

MAKES 15

225 g/8 oz self-raising flour

1 tsp baking powder

1 tsp cocoa powder, plus extra for dusting

225 g/8 oz butter, softened, plus extra for greasing

225 g/8 oz golden caster sugar

4 eggs, beaten

3 tbsp instant coffee granules, dissolved in 2 tbsp hot water, cooled

white chocolate frosting

115 g/4 oz white chocolate, broken into pieces

55 g/2 oz butter, softened

3 tbsp milk

175 g/6 oz icing sugar

BAKEWELL SLICES

For the pastry, sift the flour into a bowl and rub in the butter with your fingertips until the mixture resembles fine breadcrumbs. Stir in the sugar, then mix the egg yolk with the water and stir in to make a firm dough, adding a little more water if necessary. Wrap in clingfilm and chill in the refrigerator for about 15 minutes, until firm enough to roll out.

Preheat the oven to 200°C/400°F/Gas Mark 6. Roll out the dough and use to line a 23-cm/9-inch square tart tin or shallow cake tin. Prick the base and chill for 15 minutes.

Meanwhile, cream together the butter and sugar until pale and fluffy, then beat in the ground almonds, eggs and almond extract.

Spread the jam over the pastry base, then top with the almond mixture, spreading evenly. Sprinkle with the flaked almonds.

Bake in the preheated oven for 10 minutes, then reduce the heat to 180°C/350°F/Gas Mark 4 and bake for a further 25–30 minutes, or until the filling is golden brown and firm to the touch. Leave to cool in the tin, then cut into bars.

MAKES 12

pastry
175 g/6 oz plain flour

125 g/4½ oz butter

25 g/1 oz caster sugar

1 egg yolk

about 1 tbsp cold water

filling
115 g/4 oz unsalted butter

115 g/4 oz caster sugar

115 g/4 oz ground almonds

3 eggs, beaten

½ tsp almond extract

4 tbsp raspberry jam

2 tbsp flaked almonds

LEMON DRIZZLE BARS

Preheat the oven to 180°C/350°F/Gas Mark 4. Grease an 18-cm/7-inch square cake tin and line with non-stick baking paper.

Place the eggs, caster sugar and margarine in a mixing bowl and beat hard until smooth and fluffy. Stir in the lemon rind, then fold in the flour lightly and evenly. Stir in the milk, mixing evenly, then spoon into the prepared cake tin, smoothing level.

Bake in the preheated oven for 45–50 minutes, or until golden brown and firm to the touch. Remove from the oven and stand the tin on a wire rack.

To make the syrup, place the icing sugar and lemon juice in a small saucepan and heat gently, stirring until the sugar dissolves. Do not boil.

Prick the warm cake all over with a skewer, and spoon the hot syrup evenly over the top, allowing it to be absorbed.

Leave to cool completely in the tin, then turn out the cake, cut into 12 pieces and dust with a little icing sugar before serving.

MAKES 12

2 eggs

175 g/6 oz caster sugar

150 g/5½ oz soft margarine, plus extra for greasing

finely grated rind of 1 lemon

175 g/6 oz self-raising flour

125 ml/4 fl oz milk

icing sugar, for dusting

syrup

140 g/5 oz icing sugar

50 ml/2 fl oz fresh lemon juice

NUTTY FLAPJACKS

Preheat the oven to 180°C/350°F/Gas Mark 4. Grease a 23-cm/9-inch square cake tin.

Place the rolled oats, hazelnuts and flour in a large mixing bowl and stir together.

Place the butter, golden syrup and sugar in a saucepan over a low heat and stir until melted. Pour onto the dry ingredients and mix well. Spoon the mixture into the prepared cake tin and smooth the surface with the back of a spoon.

Bake in the preheated oven for 20–25 minutes, or until golden and firm to the touch. Mark into 16 pieces and leave to cool in the tin. When completely cold, cut with a sharp knife and remove from the tin.

MAKES 16

200 g/7 oz rolled oats

115 g/4 oz chopped hazelnuts

55 g/2 oz plain flour

115 g/4 oz butter, plus extra for greasing

2 tbsp golden syrup

85 g/3 oz light muscovado sugar

CHOCOLATE CARAMEL SHORTBREAD

Preheat the oven to 180ºC/350ºF/Gas Mark 4. Grease and line the base of a 23-cm/9-inch shallow square cake tin.

Place the butter, flour and sugar in a food processor and process until it begins to bind together. Press the mixture into the prepared tin and smooth the top. Bake in the preheated oven for 20–25 minutes, or until golden.

Meanwhile, make the filling. Place the butter, sugar, golden syrup and condensed milk in a saucepan and heat gently until the sugar has dissolved. Bring to the boil and simmer for 6–8 minutes, stirring constantly, until the mixture becomes very thick. Pour over the shortbread base and leave to chill in the refrigerator until firm.

To make the topping, melt the chocolate and leave to cool, then spread over the caramel. Chill in the refrigerator until set. Cut the shortbread into 12 pieces with a sharp knife and serve.

MAKES 12

115 g/4 oz butter, plus extra for greasing

175 g/6 oz plain flour

55 g/2 oz golden caster sugar

filling and topping

175 g/6 oz butter

115 g/4 oz golden caster sugar

3 tbsp golden syrup

400 g/14 oz canned condensed milk

200 g/7 oz plain chocolate, broken into pieces

STRAWBERRY SHORTCAKES

Preheat the oven to 180°C/350°F/Gas Mark 4. Lightly grease a large baking tray.

Sift the flour, baking powder and caster sugar into a bowl. Rub in the butter with your fingertips until the mixture resembles breadcrumbs. Beat the egg with 2 tablespoons of the milk and stir into the dry ingredients with a fork to form a soft, but not sticky, dough, adding more milk if necessary.

Turn out the dough onto a lightly floured surface and roll out to a thickness of about 2 cm/¾ inch. Stamp out rounds using a 7-cm/2¾-inch biscuit cutter. Press the trimmings together lightly and stamp out more rounds.

Place the rounds on the prepared baking tray and brush the tops lightly with milk. Bake in the preheated oven for 12–15 minutes, until firm and golden brown. Place on a wire rack to cool.

For the filling, stir the vanilla extract into the mascarpone cheese with 2 tablespoons of the icing sugar. Reserve a few whole strawberries for decoration, then hull and slice the rest. Sprinkle with the remaining tablespoon of icing sugar.

Split the shortcakes in half horizontally. Spoon half the mascarpone mixture onto the bases and top with sliced strawberries. Spoon over the remaining mascarpone mixture and replace the shortcake tops. To serve, dust with icing sugar and top with the reserved whole strawberries.

SERVES 6

225 g/8 oz self-raising flour, plus extra for dusting

½ tsp baking powder

100 g/3½ oz golden caster sugar

85 g/3 oz unsalted butter, plus extra for greasing

1 egg, beaten

2–3 tbsp milk, plus extra for brushing

filling

1 tsp vanilla extract

250 g/9 oz mascarpone cheese

3 tbsp icing sugar, plus extra for dusting

400 g/14 oz strawberries

SCONES

Preheat the oven to 220°C/425°F/Gas Mark 7.

Sift the flour, salt and baking powder into a bowl. Rub in the butter using your fingertips until the mixture resembles breadcrumbs. Stir in the sugar. Make a well in the centre and pour in the milk. Stir in using a palette knife and bring together to make a soft dough.

Turn the mixture onto a floured surface and lightly flatten the dough until it is of an even thickness, about 1 cm/½ inch. Don't be heavy-handed; scones need a light touch.

Cut out the scones using a 6-cm/2½-inch biscuit cutter and place on a baking tray.

Brush with a little milk and bake in the preheated oven for 10–12 minutes, until golden and well risen. Cool on a wire rack and serve freshly baked with strawberry jam and clotted cream.

MAKES 10–12

450 g/1 lb plain flour, plus extra for dusting

½ tsp salt

2 tsp baking powder

55 g/2 oz butter

2 tbsp caster sugar

250 ml/9 fl oz milk, plus extra for brushing

strawberry jam and clotted cream, to serve

ALMOND
MACAROONS

Preheat the oven to 180°C/350°F/Gas Mark 4. Line two baking trays with baking paper.

Beat the egg white with a fork until frothy, then stir in the ground almonds, sugar and almond extract, mixing to form a sticky dough.

Using lightly sugared hands, roll the dough into small balls and place on the prepared baking trays. Press an almond half into the centre of each.

Bake in the preheated oven for 15–20 minutes, or until pale golden. Place on a wire rack to cool.

MAKES 12–14

1 egg white

85 g/3 oz ground almonds

85 g/3 oz caster sugar, plus extra for rolling

½ tsp almond extract

6–7 blanched almonds, split in half

PIES & PASTRIES

APPLE PIE

To make the pastry, sift the flour and salt into a mixing bowl. Add the butter and lard, and rub in with your fingertips until the mixture resembles fine breadcrumbs. Add enough cold water to mix to a firm dough. Wrap in clingfilm and chill in the refrigerator for 30 minutes.

Preheat the oven to 220°C/425°F/Gas Mark 7. Roll out almost two thirds of the pastry thinly and use to line a deep 23-cm/ 9-inch pie plate.

For the filling, mix the apples with the sugar and spices, and pack into the pastry case – the filling can come up above the rim. Add the water, if needed, particularly if the apples are not very juicy.

Roll out the remaining pastry to form a lid. Dampen the edges of the pie rim with water and position the lid, pressing the edges firmly together. Trim and crimp the edges.

Use the pastry trimmings to cut out leaves or other shapes to decorate the top of the pie. Dampen and attach. Glaze the top of the pie with beaten egg or milk, make one or two slits in the top and place the pie on a baking tray.

Bake in the preheated oven for 20 minutes, then reduce the temperature to 180°C/350°F/Gas Mark 4 and bake for a further 30 minutes, or until the pastry is a light golden brown. Serve hot or cold, sprinkled with sugar.

SERVES 6–8

pastry
175 g/6 oz plain flour

pinch of salt

85 g/3 oz butter or margarine, cut into small pieces

85 g/3 oz lard or white vegetable fat, cut into small pieces

about 1–2 tbsp water

beaten egg or milk, for glazing

filling
750 g–1 kg/1 lb 10 oz–2 lb 4 oz cooking apples, peeled, cored and sliced

125 g/4½ oz soft light brown or caster sugar, plus extra for sprinkling

½–1 tsp ground cinnamon, mixed spice or ground ginger

about 1–2 tbsp water

LATTICED CHERRY PIE

To make the pastry, sift the flour and baking powder into a large bowl. Stir in the mixed spice, salt and sugar. Rub in the butter with your fingertips until the mixture resembles fine breadcrumbs. Add the beaten egg and mix to a firm dough. Cut the dough in half and roll each half into a ball. Wrap in clingfilm and chill in the refrigerator for 30 minutes.

Preheat the oven to 220°C/425°F/Gas Mark 7. Grease a 23-cm/ 9-inch round tart tin. Roll out the pastry into two 30-cm/12-inch rounds and use one to line the tart tin.

To make the filling, put half the cherries and the sugar into a large saucepan. Bring to a simmer over a low heat, stirring, for 5 minutes, or until the sugar has melted. Stir in the almond extract, brandy and mixed spice. In a separate bowl, mix the cornflour and water to form a paste. Remove the saucepan from the heat, stir in the cornflour paste, then return to the heat and stir constantly until the mixture boils and thickens. Leave to cool a little. Stir in the remaining cherries, pour into the pastry case, then dot with the butter.

Cut the remaining pastry round into long strips about 1 cm/ ½ inch wide. Lay five strips evenly across the top of the filling in the same direction. Now lay six strips crossways over the strips, folding under every other strip to form a lattice. Trim off the edges and seal with water. Use your fingers to crimp around the rim, then brush the top with beaten egg. Cover with foil, then bake in the preheated oven for 30 minutes. Discard the foil, then bake for a further 15 minutes, or until golden.

SERVES 8

pastry

140 g/5 oz plain flour, plus extra for dusting

¼ tsp baking powder

½ tsp mixed spice

½ tsp salt

50 g/1¾ oz caster sugar

55 g/2 oz cold unsalted butter, diced, plus extra for greasing

1 egg, beaten, plus extra for glazing

filling

900 g/2 lb stoned fresh cherries, or canned cherries, drained

150 g/5 oz caster sugar

½ tsp almond extract

2 tsp cherry brandy

¼ tsp mixed spice

2 tbsp cornflour

2 tbsp water

25 g/1 oz butter

PEAR TART WITH CHOCOLATE SAUCE

Preheat the oven to 200°C/400°F/Gas Mark 6. Lightly grease a 20-cm/8-inch round tart tin.

Sift the flour into a mixing bowl and stir in the ground almonds. Rub in the margarine with your fingertips until the mixture resembles breadcrumbs. Add enough water to mix to a soft dough. Cover, chill in the freezer for 10 minutes, then roll out and use to line the prepared tin. Prick the base with a fork and chill again.

To make the filling, beat the butter and sugar until light and fluffy. Beat in the eggs, then fold in the ground almonds, cocoa powder and almond extract. Spread the chocolate mixture in the pastry case. Thinly slice each pear widthways, flatten slightly, then arrange the pears on top of the chocolate mixture, pressing down lightly. Bake in the preheated oven for 30 minutes, or until the filling has risen. Cool slightly and transfer to a serving plate, if wished.

To make the chocolate sauce, place the sugar, golden syrup and water in a saucepan and heat gently, stirring until the sugar dissolves. Boil gently for 1 minute. Remove from the heat, add the chocolate and butter and stir until melted and well combined. Serve with the tart.

SERVES 6

100 g/3½ oz plain flour

25 g/1 oz ground almonds

60 g/2¼ oz block margarine, plus extra for greasing

about 3 tbsp water

filling

50 g/1¾ oz butter

50 g/1¾ oz caster sugar

2 eggs, beaten

100 g/3½ oz ground almonds

2 tbsp cocoa powder

a few drops of almond extract

400 g/14 oz canned pear halves in natural juice, drained

chocolate sauce

4 tbsp caster sugar

3 tbsp golden syrup

100 ml/3½ fl oz water

175 g/6 oz plain chocolate, broken into pieces

25 g/1 oz butter

LEMON MERINGUE PIE

To make the pastry, sift the flour into a bowl. Rub in the butter with your fingertips until the mixture resembles fine breadcrumbs. Mix in the remaining ingredients. Knead briefly on a lightly floured work surface. Wrap in clingfilm and chill in the refrigerator for 30 minutes.

Preheat the oven to 180°C/350°F/Gas Mark 4. Grease a 20-cm/8-inch round tart tin. Roll out the pastry to a thickness of 5 mm/¼ inch, then use it to line the base and sides of the tin. Prick all over with a fork, line with baking paper and fill with baking beans. Bake in the preheated oven for 15 minutes. Remove the pastry case from the oven and take out the paper and beans. Reduce the temperature to 150°C/300°F/Gas Mark 2.

For the filling, mix the cornflour with a little of the water to form a paste. Put the remaining water in a saucepan. Stir in the lemon juice and rind and cornflour paste. Bring to the boil, stirring. Cook for 2 minutes. Cool a little. Stir in five tablespoons of the caster sugar and the egg yolks, and pour into the pastry case.

Whisk the egg whites in a clean, grease-free bowl until stiff. Gradually whisk in the remaining caster sugar and spread over the pie. Bake for a further 40 minutes. Remove from the oven, cool and serve.

SERVES 6–8

pastry

150 g/5½ oz plain flour, plus extra for dusting

85 g/3 oz butter, cut into small pieces, plus extra for greasing

35 g/1¼ oz icing sugar, sifted

finely grated rind of ½ lemon

½ egg yolk, beaten

1½ tbsp milk

filling

3 tbsp cornflour

300 ml/10 fl oz water

juice and grated rind of 2 lemons

175 g/6 oz caster sugar

2 eggs, separated

SWEET
PUMPKIN PIE

Preheat the oven to 190ºC/375ºF/Gas Mark 5. Put the pumpkin halves, face down, in a shallow baking tin and cover with foil. Bake in the preheated oven for 1½ hours, then leave to cool. Scoop out the flesh and purée in a food processor. Drain off any excess liquid. Cover and chill.

Grease a 23-cm/9-inch round tart tin. To make the pastry, sift the flour and baking powder into a large bowl. Stir in ½ teaspoon of the cinnamon, ¼ teaspoon of the nutmeg, ¼ teaspoon of the cloves, ½ teaspoon of the salt and all the caster sugar. Rub in the butter with your fingertips until the mixture resembles fine breadcrumbs, then make a well in the centre. Lightly beat one of the eggs and pour it into the well. Mix together with a wooden spoon, then shape the dough into a ball. Place the dough on a lightly floured surface, roll out and use to line the prepared tin. Trim the edges, then cover and chill for 30 minutes.

Preheat the oven to 220ºC/425ºF/Gas Mark 7. Put the pumpkin purée in a large bowl, then stir in the condensed milk and the remaining eggs. Add the remaining spices and salt, then stir in the vanilla extract and demerara sugar. Pour into the pastry case and bake in the preheated oven for 15 minutes.

Meanwhile, make the topping. Mix the flour, demerara sugar and cinnamon in a bowl, rub in the butter, then stir in the nuts. Remove the pie from the oven and reduce the heat to 180ºC/350ºF/Gas Mark 4. Sprinkle over the topping, then bake for a further 35 minutes.

SERVES 6

- 1.8 kg/4 lb sweet pumpkin, halved and deseeded, stem and stringy bits removed
- 140 g/5 oz plain flour, plus extra for dusting
- ¼ tsp baking powder
- 1½ tsp ground cinnamon
- ¾ tsp ground nutmeg
- ¾ tsp ground cloves
- 1 tsp salt
- 50 g/1¾ oz caster sugar
- 55 g/2 oz cold unsalted butter, diced, plus extra for greasing
- 3 eggs
- 400 ml/14 fl oz canned condensed milk
- ½ tsp vanilla extract
- 1 tbsp demerara sugar

streusel topping
- 2 tbsp plain flour
- 4 tbsp demerara sugar
- 1 tsp ground cinnamon
- 2 tbsp cold unsalted butter, diced
- 75 g/2¾ oz pecan nuts, chopped
- 75 g/2¾ oz walnuts, chopped

PECAN PIE

For the pastry, place the flour in a bowl and rub in the butter with your fingertips until it resembles fine breadcrumbs. Stir in the caster sugar and add enough cold water to mix to a firm dough. Wrap in clingfilm and chill for 15 minutes, until firm enough to roll out.

Preheat the oven to 200°C/400°F/Gas Mark 6. Roll out the pastry on a lightly floured surface and use to line a 23-cm/ 9-inch loose-based round tart tin. Prick the base with a fork. Chill for 15 minutes.

Place the tart tin on a baking tray and line with a sheet of baking paper and baking beans. Bake blind in the preheated oven for 10 minutes. Remove the baking beans and paper and bake for a further 5 minutes. Reduce the oven temperature to 180°C/350°F/Gas Mark 4.

For the filling, place the butter, muscovado sugar and golden syrup in a saucepan and heat gently until melted. Remove from the heat and quickly beat in the eggs and vanilla extract.

Roughly chop the pecans and stir into the mixture. Pour into the pastry case and bake for 35–40 minutes, until the filling is just set. Serve warm or cold.

SERVES 8

pastry

200 g/7 oz plain flour, plus extra for dusting

115 g/4 oz unsalted butter

2 tbsp caster sugar

a little cold water

filling

70 g/2½ oz unsalted butter

100 g/3½ oz light muscovado sugar

140 g/5 oz golden syrup

2 large eggs, beaten

1 tsp vanilla extract

115 g/4 oz pecan nuts

MISSISSIPPI
MUD PIE

To make the pastry, sift the flour and cocoa powder into a mixing bowl. Rub in the butter with your fingertips until the mixture resembles fine breadcrumbs. Stir in the sugar and enough cold water to mix to a soft dough. Wrap the dough in clingfilm and chill in the refrigerator for 15 minutes.

Preheat the oven to 190°C/375°F/Gas Mark 5. Roll out the pastry on a lightly floured work surface and use to line a 23-cm/ 9-inch loose-based round tart tin. Line with baking paper and fill with baking beans. Bake in the preheated oven for 15 minutes. Remove the paper and beans from the pastry case and cook for a further 10 minutes, until crisp.

To make the filling, beat the butter and sugar together in a bowl and gradually beat in the eggs with the cocoa powder. Place the chocolate in a heatproof bowl set over a saucepan of gently simmering water until melted. Beat the melted chocolate into the butter mixture with the single cream and chocolate extract.

Reduce the oven temperature to 160°C/325°F/Gas Mark 3. Pour the mixture into the pastry case and bake for 45 minutes, or until the filling has set gently.

Leave to cool completely, then transfer the pie to a serving plate. Cover with the whipped cream and decorate with chocolate flakes and curls, then chill until ready to serve.

SERVES 8

pastry
225 g/8 oz plain flour, plus extra for dusting

2 tbsp cocoa powder

140 g/5 oz butter

2 tbsp caster sugar

1–2 tbsp cold water

filling
175 g/6 oz butter

350 g/12 oz soft dark brown sugar

4 eggs, lightly beaten

4 tbsp cocoa powder, sifted

150 g/5½ oz plain chocolate, broken into pieces

300 ml/10 fl oz single cream

1 tsp chocolate extract

to decorate
425 ml/15 fl oz double cream, whipped

chocolate flakes and curls

CHOCOLATE ÉCLAIRS

Preheat the oven to 200°C/400°F/Gas Mark 6. Lightly grease a baking tray.

Place the water in a saucepan, add the butter and heat gently until the butter melts. Bring to a rolling boil, then remove the saucepan from the heat and add the flour all at once, beating well until the mixture leaves the sides of the saucepan and forms a ball. Leave to cool slightly, then gradually beat in the eggs to form a smooth, glossy mixture. Spoon into a large piping bag fitted with a 1-cm/½-inch plain nozzle.

Sprinkle the baking tray with a little water. Pipe éclairs 7.5 cm/ 3 inches long, spaced well apart. Bake in the preheated oven for 30–35 minutes, or until crisp and golden. Make a small slit in the side of each éclair to let the steam escape, then leave to cool on a wire rack.

Meanwhile, make the pastry cream. Whisk the eggs and caster sugar until thick and creamy, then fold in the cornflour. Heat the milk until almost boiling and pour onto the egg mixture, whisking. Transfer to the saucepan and cook over a low heat, stirring until thick. Remove the saucepan from the heat and stir in the vanilla extract. Cover and leave to cool.

To make the icing, melt the butter with the milk in a saucepan, remove from the heat and stir in the cocoa and icing sugar. Split the éclairs lengthways and pipe in the pastry cream. Spread the icing over the top of the éclairs. Melt a little white chocolate in a heatproof bowl set over a saucepan of gently simmering water, then drizzle over the chocolate icing and leave to set.

MAKES 12

choux pastry
150 ml/5 fl oz water

70 g/2½ oz butter, diced, plus extra for greasing

100 g/3½ oz plain flour, sifted

2 eggs

pastry cream
2 eggs, lightly beaten

4 tbsp caster sugar

2 tbsp cornflour

300 ml/10 fl oz milk

¼ tsp vanilla extract

icing
2 tbsp butter

1 tbsp milk

1 tbsp cocoa powder

55 g/2 oz icing sugar

50 g/1¾ oz white chocolate, broken into pieces

STRAWBERRY
PETITS CHOUX

Sprinkle the gelatine over the water in a heatproof bowl. Let it soften for 2 minutes. Place the bowl over a saucepan of simmering water and stir until the gelatine dissolves. Remove from the heat.

Place 225 g/8 oz of the strawberries in a blender with the ricotta, sugar and liqueur. Process until blended. Add the gelatine and process briefly. Transfer the mousse to a bowl, cover with clingfilm and chill for 1–1½ hours, until set.

Preheat the oven to 220°C/425°F/Gas Mark 7. Line a baking tray with baking paper.

To make the petits choux, sift together the flour, cocoa powder and salt. Put the butter and water into a heavy-based saucepan and heat gently until the butter has melted. Remove the saucepan from the heat and add the flour mixture all at once, stirring well until the mixture leaves the sides of the saucepan. Leave to cool slightly.Gradually beat the eggs and egg white into the flour paste and continue beating until it is smooth and glossy. Drop 12 rounded tablespoonfuls of the mixture onto the prepared baking tray and bake in the preheated oven for 20–25 minutes, until puffed up and crisp. Remove from the oven and make a small slit in the side of each petit chou. Return to the oven for 5 minutes. Transfer to a wire rack.

Slice the remaining strawberries. Cut the petits choux in half, divide the mousse and strawberry slices between them, then replace the tops. Dust lightly with icing sugar and place in the refrigerator. Serve within 1½ hours.

MAKES 12

filling and topping
2 tsp powdered gelatine

2 tbsp water

350 g/12 oz strawberries

225 g/8 oz ricotta cheese

1 tbsp caster sugar

2 tsp crème de fraises de bois
   liqueur

icing sugar, for dusting

petits choux
100 g/3½ oz plain flour

2 tbsp cocoa powder

pinch of salt

6 tbsp unsalted butter

225 ml/8 fl oz water

2 eggs, plus 1 egg white, beaten

SHORTBREAD

Preheat the oven to 150°C/300°F/Gas Mark 2. Grease a 20-cm/ 8-inch fluted round tart tin.

Mix together the flour, salt and sugar. Rub the butter into the dry ingredients. Continue to work the mixture until it forms a soft dough. Make sure you do not overwork the shortbread or it will be tough, not crumbly as it should be.

Lightly press the dough into the prepared tart tin. If you don't have a fluted tin, roll out the dough on a lightly floured board, place on a baking tray and pinch the edges to form a scalloped pattern.

Mark into eight pieces with a knife. Prick all over with a fork and bake in the preheated oven for 45–50 minutes, until the shortbread is firm and just coloured.

Leave to cool in the tin and sprinkle with the sugar. Cut into portions and remove to a wire rack to cool.

MAKES 8

175 g/6 oz plain flour, plus extra for dusting

pinch of salt

55 g/2 oz caster sugar, plus extra for sprinkling

115 g/4 oz butter, cut into small pieces, plus extra for greasing

CITRUS
CRESCENTS

Preheat the oven to 200°C/400°F/Gas Mark 6. Lightly grease two baking trays.

In a mixing bowl, cream together the butter and sugar until light and fluffy, then gradually beat in the egg yolk.

Sift the flour into the creamed mixture and mix until evenly combined. Add the orange, lemon and lime rinds to the mixture with enough of the orange juice to make a soft dough.

Roll out the dough on a lightly floured surface. Stamp out rounds using a 7.5-cm/3-inch biscuit cutter. Make crescent shapes by cutting away a quarter of each round. Re-roll the trimmings to make about 25 crescents.

Place the crescents on the prepared baking trays. Prick the surface of each crescent with a fork. Lightly whisk the egg white in a small bowl and brush it over the biscuits.

Bake in the preheated oven for 12–15 minutes. Leave the biscuits to cool on a wire rack before serving.

MAKES ABOUT 25

100 g/3½ oz butter, softened, plus extra for greasing

75 g/2¾ oz caster sugar

1 egg, separated

200 g/7 oz plain flour, plus extra for dusting

grated rind of 1 orange

grated rind of 1 lemon

grated rind of 1 lime

2–3 tbsp orange juice

VANILLA
HEARTS

Preheat the oven to 180°C/350°F/Gas Mark 4, then lightly grease a baking tray.

Sift the flour into a large bowl. Add the butter and rub it in with your fingertips until the mixture resembles fine breadcrumbs. Stir in the sugar and vanilla extract and mix together to form a firm dough.

Roll out the dough on a lightly floured work surface to a thickness of 1 cm/½ inch. Stamp out 12 hearts with a heart-shaped biscuit cutter measuring about 5 cm/2 inches across. Arrange the hearts on the prepared baking tray.

Bake in the preheated oven for 15–20 minutes, or until just coloured. Transfer to a wire rack and leave to cool completely. Dust with a little caster sugar just before serving.

MAKES 12

225 g/8 oz plain flour, plus extra for dusting

150 g/5½ oz butter, cut into small pieces, plus extra for greasing

125 g/4½ oz caster sugar, plus extra for dusting

1 tsp vanilla extract

GINGERBREAD PEOPLE

Preheat the oven to 160°C/325°F/Gas Mark 3, then grease three large baking trays.

Sift the flour, ginger, mixed spice and bicarbonate of soda into a large bowl. Place the butter, golden syrup and muscovado sugar in a saucepan over a low heat and stir until melted. Pour onto the dry ingredients and add the egg. Mix together to make a dough. The dough will be sticky to start with, but will become firmer as it cools.

On a lightly floured work surface, roll out the dough to about 3 mm/⅛ inch thick and stamp out gingerbread people shapes. Place on the prepared baking trays. Re-knead and re-roll the trimmings and cut out more shapes. Decorate with currants for eyes and pieces of glacé cherry for mouths. Bake in the preheated oven for 15–20 minutes, or until firm and lightly browned.

Remove from the oven and leave to cool on the baking trays for a few minutes, then transfer to wire racks to cool completely.

Mix the icing sugar with the water to a thick consistency. Place the icing in a small piping bag fitted with a plain nozzle and use to pipe buttons or bows onto the cooled biscuits.

MAKES 20

450 g/1 lb plain flour, plus extra for dusting

2 tsp ground ginger

1 tsp ground mixed spice

2 tsp bicarbonate of soda

115 g/4 oz butter, plus extra for greasing

100 g/3½ oz golden syrup

115 g/4 oz light muscovado sugar

1 egg, beaten

to decorate

currants

glacé cherries

85 g/3 oz icing sugar

3–4 tsp water

CHEQUERBOARD COOKIES

Put the butter and sugar into a bowl and mix well with a wooden spoon, then beat in the egg yolk and vanilla extract. Sift together the flour and salt into the mixture and stir until thoroughly combined.

Divide the dough in half. Add the ginger and orange rind to one half and mix well. Shape the dough into a log 15 cm/ 6 inches long. Flatten the sides and top to square off the log to 5 cm/2 inches high. Wrap in clingfilm and chill in the refrigerator for 30–60 minutes. Add the cocoa to the other half of the dough and mix well. Shape into a flattened log exactly the same size as the first one, wrap in clingfilm and chill in the refrigerator for 30–60 minutes.

Unwrap the dough and cut each flattened log lengthways into three slices. Cut each slice lengthways into three strips. Brush the strips with egg white and stack them in threes, alternating the colours, so they are the same shape as the original logs. Wrap in clingfilm and chill in the refrigerator for 30–60 minutes.

Preheat the oven to 190°C/375°F/Gas Mark 5. Line two baking trays with baking paper.

Unwrap the logs and cut into slices with a sharp serrated knife. Put the cookies on the prepared baking trays, spaced well apart. Bake in the preheated oven for 12–15 minutes, until firm. Leave to cool for 5–10 minutes, then carefully transfer to wire racks to cool completely.

MAKES ABOUT 20

225 g/8 oz butter, softened

140 g/5 oz caster sugar

1 egg yolk, lightly beaten

2 tsp vanilla extract

280 g/10 oz plain flour

pinch of salt

1 tsp ground ginger

1 tbsp finely grated orange rind

1 tbsp cocoa powder, sifted

1 egg white, lightly beaten

VIENNESE FINGERS

Preheat the oven to 160°C/325°F/Gas Mark 3. Lightly grease two baking trays.

Place the butter, sugar and vanilla extract in a bowl and cream together until pale and fluffy. Stir in the flour, mixing evenly to a fairly stiff dough.

Place the mixture in a piping bag fitted with a large star nozzle and pipe about 16 fingers, each 6 cm/2½ inches long, onto the prepared baking trays.

Bake in the preheated oven for 10–15 minutes, until pale golden. Cool for 2–3 minutes on the baking trays, then lift carefully onto a cooling rack with a palette knife to finish cooling.

Place the chocolate in a small heatproof bowl over a pan of gently simmering water until melted. Remove from the heat. Dip the ends of each biscuit into the chocolate to coat, then place on a sheet of baking paper and leave to set.

MAKES ABOUT 16

100 g/3½ oz unsalted butter, plus extra for greasing

25 g/1 oz golden caster sugar

½ tsp vanilla extract

100 g/3½ oz self-raising flour

100 g/3½ oz plain chocolate

BRANDY SNAPS

Preheat the oven to 160°C/325°F/Gas Mark 3. Line three large baking trays with baking paper.

Place the butter, sugar and golden syrup in a saucepan and heat gently over a low heat, stirring occasionally, until melted. Remove from the heat and leave to cool slightly. Sift the flour and ginger into the pan and beat until smooth, then stir in the brandy and lemon rind.

Drop small spoonfuls of the mixture onto the prepared baking trays, leaving plenty of room for spreading. Place one baking tray at a time in the preheated oven for 10–12 minutes, or until the snaps are golden brown.

Remove the first baking tray from the oven and leave to cool for about 30 seconds, then lift each round with a palette knife and wrap around the handle of a wooden spoon. If the brandy snaps start to become too firm to wrap, return them to the oven for about 30 seconds to soften again. When firm, remove from the spoon handles and finish cooling on a wire rack. Repeat with the remaining baking trays.

For the filling, whip the cream with the brandy and icing sugar until thick. Just before serving, pipe the cream mixture into each end of the brandy snaps.

MAKES ABOUT 20

85 g/3 oz unsalted butter

85 g/3 oz golden caster sugar

3 tbsp golden syrup

85 g/3 oz plain flour

1 tsp ground ginger

1 tbsp brandy

finely grated rind of ½ lemon

filling

150 ml/5 fl oz double cream or whipping cream

1 tbsp brandy (optional)

1 tbsp icing sugar

PISTACHIO & ALMOND TUILES

Preheat the oven to 160°C/325°F/Gas Mark 3. Line two baking trays with baking paper.

Whisk the egg white lightly with the sugar, then stir in the flour, pistachios, ground almonds, almond extract and butter, mixing to a soft paste.

Place walnut-sized spoonfuls of the mixture on the prepared baking trays and use the back of the spoon to spread as thinly as possible. Bake in the preheated oven for 10–15 minutes, until pale golden.

Quickly lift each biscuit with a palette knife and place over the side of a rolling pin to shape into a curve. When set, transfer to a wire rack to cool.

MAKES 12

1 egg white

55 g/2 oz golden caster sugar

25 g/1 oz plain flour

25 g/1 oz pistachio nuts, finely chopped

25 g/1 oz ground almonds

1/2 tsp almond extract

40 g/1½ oz unsalted butter, melted and cooled

MINI FLORENTINES

Preheat the oven to 180°C/350°F/Gas Mark 4. Line two baking trays with baking paper.

Place the butter in a small saucepan and heat gently until melted. Add the sugar, stir until dissolved, then bring the mixture to the boil. Remove from the heat and stir in the sultanas, glacé cherries, glacé ginger, sunflower seeds and almonds. Mix well, then beat in the cream.

Place small teaspoons of mixture onto the prepared baking trays, allowing plenty of space for the mixture to spread during baking. Bake in the preheated oven for 10–12 minutes, or until light golden in colour.

Remove from the oven and, while still hot, use a round biscuit cutter to pull in the edges to form perfect circles. Leave to cool and go crisp before removing from the baking trays.

Put the chocolate in a heatproof bowl set over a saucepan of gently simmering water and stir until melted. Spread most of the chocolate onto a sheet of baking paper. When the chocolate is on the point of setting, place the biscuits flat-side down on the chocolate and let it harden completely.

Cut around the florentines and remove from the baking paper. Spread the remaining melted chocolate on the coated side of the florentines and use a fork to mark waves in the chocolate. Leave to set.

MAKES 40

75 g/2¾ oz butter

75 g/2¾ oz caster sugar

25 g/1 oz sultanas or raisins

25 g/1 oz glacé cherries, chopped

25 g/1 oz glacé ginger, chopped

25 g/1 oz sunflower seeds

100 g/3½ oz flaked almonds

2 tbsp double cream

175 g/6 oz plain or milk chocolate, broken into pieces

CHEQUERBOARD COOKIES

Put the butter and sugar into a bowl and mix well with a wooden spoon, then beat in the egg yolk and vanilla extract. Sift together the flour and salt into the mixture and stir until thoroughly combined.

Divide the dough in half. Add the ginger and orange rind to one half and mix well. Shape the dough into a log 15 cm/ 6 inches long. Flatten the sides and top to square off the log to 5 cm/2 inches high. Wrap in clingfilm and chill in the refrigerator for 30–60 minutes. Add the cocoa to the other half of the dough and mix well. Shape into a flattened log exactly the same size as the first one, wrap in clingfilm and chill in the refrigerator for 30–60 minutes.

Unwrap the dough and cut each flattened log lengthways into three slices. Cut each slice lengthways into three strips. Brush the strips with egg white and stack them in threes, alternating the colours, so they are the same shape as the original logs. Wrap in clingfilm and chill in the refrigerator for 30–60 minutes.

Preheat the oven to 190°C/375°F/Gas Mark 5. Line two baking trays with baking paper.

Unwrap the logs and cut into slices with a sharp serrated knife. Put the cookies on the prepared baking trays, spaced well apart. Bake in the preheated oven for 12–15 minutes, until firm. Leave to cool for 5–10 minutes, then carefully transfer to wire racks to cool completely.

MAKES ABOUT 20

225 g/8 oz butter, softened

140 g/5 oz caster sugar

1 egg yolk, lightly beaten

2 tsp vanilla extract

280 g/10 oz plain flour

pinch of salt

1 tsp ground ginger

1 tbsp finely grated orange rind

1 tbsp cocoa powder, sifted

1 egg white, lightly beaten

ALMOND
BISCOTTI

Preheat the oven to 180°C/350°F/Gas Mark 4, then lightly dust a baking tray with flour.

Sift the flour, baking powder and salt into a bowl. Add the sugar, eggs and orange rind and mix to a dough. Knead in the almonds.

Roll the dough into a ball, cut in half and roll out each portion into a log about 4 cm/1½ inches in diameter. Place the logs on the prepared baking tray and then bake in the preheated oven for 10 minutes. Remove from the oven and leave to cool for 5 minutes.

Using a serrated knife, cut the logs into 1 cm/½ inch thick diagonal slices. Arrange the slices on the baking tray and return to the oven for 15 minutes, or until slightly golden. Transfer to a wire rack to cool and go crisp.

MAKES 20–24

250 g/9 oz plain flour, plus extra for dusting

1 tsp baking powder

pinch of salt

150 g/5½ oz golden caster sugar

2 eggs, beaten

finely grated rind of 1 orange

100 g/3½ oz whole blanched almonds, lightly toasted

BREAD & SAVOURY

CRUSTY WHITE BREAD

BREAD & SAVOURY

162

Place the egg and egg yolk in a jug and beat lightly to mix. Add enough lukewarm water to make up to 300 ml/10 fl oz. Stir well.

Place the flour, salt, sugar and yeast in a large bowl. Add the butter and rub it in with your fingertips until the mixture resembles breadcrumbs. Make a well in the centre, add the egg mixture and work to a smooth dough.

Turn out onto a lightly floured surface and knead well for about 10 minutes, until smooth. Brush a bowl with oil. Shape the dough into a ball, place it in the bowl and cover with a damp tea towel. Leave to rise in a warm place for 1 hour, until the dough has doubled in volume.

Preheat the oven to 220°C/425°F/Gas Mark 7. Oil a 900-g/ 2-lb loaf tin. Turn out the dough onto a lightly floured surface and knead for 1 minute until smooth. Shape the dough the length of the tin and three times the width. Fold the dough into three lengthways and place it in the tin with the join underneath. Cover and leave in a warm place for 30 minutes, until it has risen above the tin.

Place in the preheated oven and bake for 30 minutes, or until firm and golden brown. Test that the loaf is cooked by tapping on the base with your knuckles – it should sound hollow. Transfer to a wire rack to cool.

MAKES 1 LOAF

1 egg

1 egg yolk

150–200 ml/5–7 fl oz lukewarm water

500 g/1 lb 2 oz strong white flour, plus extra for dusting

1½ tsp salt

2 tsp sugar

1 tsp easy-blend dried yeast

25 g/1 oz butter, diced

sunflower oil, for greasing

CORIANDER & GARLIC NAAN

Sift the flour, salt and ground coriander together into a bowl and stir in the garlic and yeast. Make a well in the centre and pour in the honey, water, yogurt and oil. Stir well with a wooden spoon until the dough begins to come together, then knead with your hands until it leaves the side of the bowl. Turn out onto a lightly floured surface and knead well for about 10 minutes, until smooth and elastic.

Brush a bowl with oil. Shape the dough into a ball, put it in the bowl and cover with a damp tea towel. Leave to rise in a warm place for 1–2 hours, until the dough has doubled in volume.

Put three baking trays in the oven and preheat to 240°C/475°F/ Gas Mark 9. Preheat the grill. Turn out the dough onto a lightly floured surface and knock back with your fist. Divide the dough into three pieces, shape each piece into a ball and cover two of them with oiled clingfilm.

Roll out the uncovered piece of dough into a teardrop shape about 8 mm/⅜ inch thick and cover with oiled clingfilm. Roll out the other pieces of dough in the same way. Place the naan on the preheated baking trays and sprinkle with the onion seeds and chopped coriander. Bake in the preheated oven for 5 minutes, until puffed up. Transfer the naan bread to the grill pan, brush with oil and grill for 2–3 minutes. Serve warm.

MAKES 3

280 g/10 oz strong white flour, plus extra for dusting

1 tsp salt

1 tbsp ground coriander

1 garlic clove, very finely chopped

1 tsp easy-blend dried yeast

2 tsp clear honey

100 ml/3½ fl oz lukewarm water

4 tbsp natural yogurt

1 tbsp vegetable oil, plus extra for brushing

1 tsp black onion seeds

1 tbsp chopped fresh coriander

BASIC PIZZA DOUGH

Sift the flour and salt together into a bowl and stir in the yeast. Make a well in the centre and pour in the oil and lukewarm water. Stir well with a wooden spoon until the dough begins to come together, then knead with your hands until it leaves the side of the bowl. Turn out onto a lightly floured surface and knead well for 5–10 minutes, until smooth and elastic.

Brush a bowl with oil. Shape the dough into a ball, put it in the bowl and cover with a damp tea towel. Leave to rise in a warm place for 1 hour, until the dough has doubled in volume.

Brush a baking tray with oil. Turn out the dough onto a lightly floured surface, knock back with your fist and knead for 1 minute. Roll or press out the dough to a 25-cm/10-inch round. Place on the prepared baking tray and push up the edge slightly all round. Cover the baking tray with a damp tea towel and leave to rise in a warm place for 10 minutes.

Preheat the oven to 200°C/400°F/Gas Mark 6. Spread the tomato sauce, if using, over the pizza base almost to the edge. If using fresh tomatoes, squeeze out some of the juice and roughly chop the flesh. Spread them evenly over the pizza base and drizzle with oil. Sprinkle the garlic over the tomato, add the cheese, sprinkle with the oregano and season with salt and pepper. Bake in the preheated oven for 15–20 minutes, until the crust is golden brown and crisp. Brush the crust with oil, garnish with basil sprigs and serve immediately.

SERVES 2–4

175 g/6 oz plain flour, plus extra for dusting

1 tsp salt

1 tsp easy-blend dried yeast

1 tbsp olive oil, plus extra for brushing and drizzling

6 tbsp lukewarm water

topping

175 ml/6 fl oz ready-made pizza tomato sauce or 350 g/12 oz tomatoes, peeled and halved

1 garlic clove, thinly sliced

55 g/2 oz mozzarella cheese, thinly sliced

1 tsp dried oregano

salt and pepper

fresh basil sprigs, to garnish

ENGLISH MUFFINS

Sift the flour and salt together into a bowl and stir in the sugar and yeast. Make a well in the centre and add the water and yogurt. Stir with a wooden spoon until the dough begins to come together, then knead with your hands until it comes away from the side of the bowl. Turn out onto a lightly floured surface and knead for 5–10 minutes, until smooth and elastic.

Brush a bowl with oil. Shape the dough into a ball, put it in the bowl and cover with a damp tea towel. Leave to rise in a warm place for 30–40 minutes, until the dough has doubled in volume.

Dust a baking tray with flour. Turn out the dough onto a lightly floured surface and knead lightly. Roll out to a thickness of 2 cm/¾ inch. Stamp out 10–12 rounds with a 7.5-cm/3-inch biscuit cutter and sprinkle each round with semolina. Transfer the muffins to the prepared baking tray, cover with a damp tea towel and leave to rise in a warm place for 30–40 minutes.

Heat a griddle or large frying pan over a medium–high heat and brush lightly with oil. Add half the muffins and cook for 7–8 minutes on each side, until golden brown. Cook the remaining muffins in the same way.

MAKES 10–12

450 g/1 lb strong white bread flour, plus extra for dusting

½ tsp salt

1 tsp caster sugar

1½ tsp easy-blend dried yeast

250 ml/9 fl oz lukewarm water

125 ml/4 fl oz natural yogurt

vegetable oil, for brushing

40 g/1½ oz semolina

QUICHE LORRAINE

For the pastry, sift the flour into a bowl and rub in the butter with your fingertips until the mixture resembles fine breadcrumbs. Stir in just enough water to bind the mixture to a firm dough.

Roll out the dough on a lightly floured surface to a round slightly larger than a 23-cm/9-inch loose-based round tart tin, 3 cm/1¼ inches deep. Lift the pastry onto the tin and press it down into the fluted edge, using the back of your finger. Roll the rolling pin over the edge of the tin to trim off the excess pastry. Prick the base all over with a fork. Chill in the refrigerator for at least 10 minutes to allow the pastry to rest and prevent shrinkage.

Preheat the oven to 200°C/400°C/Gas Mark 6 and preheat a baking tray. Place a sheet of baking paper in the pastry-lined tin. Fill with baking beans to weigh it down. Place on the baking tray and bake in the preheated oven for 10 minutes. Remove the paper and beans and bake for a further 10 minutes.

For the filling, melt the butter in a frying pan and cook the onion and bacon over a medium heat for about 5 minutes, stirring occasionally, until the onion is softened and lightly browned. Spread the mixture evenly in the hot pastry case and sprinkle with half the cheese. Beat together the eggs and cream in a small bowl and season to taste with pepper. Pour into the pastry case and sprinkle with the remaining cheese.

Reduce the oven temperature to 190°C/375°F/Gas Mark 5. Place the quiche in the oven and bake for 25–30 minutes, or until golden brown and just set. Cool for 10 minutes before turning out.

SERVES 4

pastry
200 g/7 oz plain flour, plus extra for dusting

100 g/3½ oz salted butter

1–2 tbsp cold water

filling
15 g/½ oz butter

1 small onion, finely chopped

4 lean streaky bacon rashers, diced

55 g/2 oz Gruyère cheese or Cheddar cheese, grated

2 eggs, beaten

300 ml/10 fl oz single cream

pepper

INDEX